ROMANCING
KERALA

SALIM PUSHPANATH

Presented by
CGH Earth
India

ROMANCING
KERALA

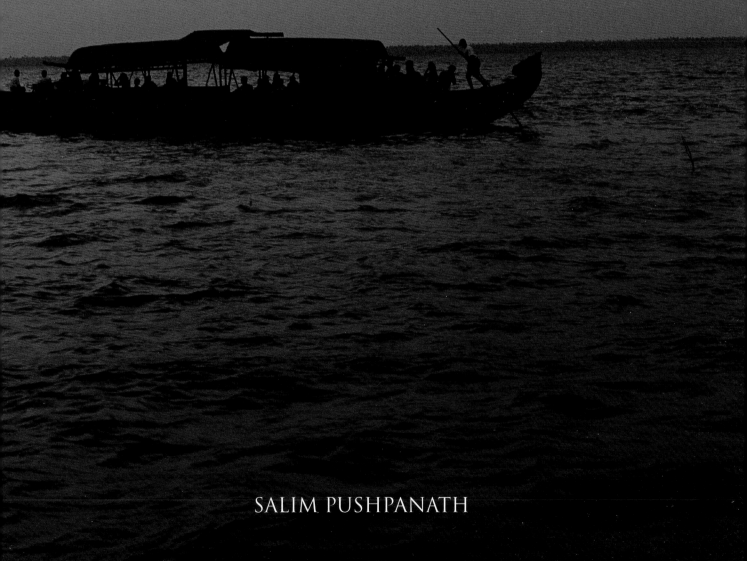

SALIM PUSHPANATH

Romancing Kerala

Concept and Photography by
Salim Pushpanath

Editorial inputs from MKS Panicker
Cover Title by Kitchu
Designed by Shaji Joseph
Images scanned by Brijilal
Pre-press by Colortone, Cochin, India.
Printed at Times Offset (M) Sdn. Bhd.

ISBN 81-88000-00-0

Published by Salim Pushpanath
DEE BEE Info Publications
Pushpanath
Kottayam 686 041
Kerala, India.

Phones: +91.481.2302799 and
+91.481.2391429
e-mail: info@salimpushpanath.com
www.salimpushpanath.com

Printed in Malaysia

Price: India Rs. 450/-

Mangalore

Karnataka

48

17

Kasaragod

Kushalnagar

Bakel

Madikeri

Mysore

Virajpet

Thaliparamba

Periya

Kannur

Sultan Bathery

Gundelpet

Thalassery

Kalpetta

Mahe

Vaythiri

Bandipur

Sathyamangalam

Gudalur

Kotagiri

Vadakara

Nilambur

Ooty

Tamil Nadu

Quilandi

Coonoor

Mettupalayam

✈ **Kozhikode**

Manjeri

Palladam

Malapuram

Coimbatore

Perinthalmanna

Shoranur

Ponnani

Palakkad

Kolongode

Pollachi

Udumalpet

ARABIAN SEA

Guruvayur

Parambikulam

Valparai

Chalakudy

Angamali

Kodungallur

Kaladi

Munnar

Paravoor

Malayattur

Some places in Kerala seem to be known by two names: for example, the state capital used to be known in English as Trivandrum, and as THIRUVANANTHAPURAM in the vernacular Malayalam.

Aluva

Kothamangalam

Painavu

✈ **Cochin**

🚢

Marari Beach

Thekkady

Vaikom

These days, the government officials and the media for chauvinistic reasons seem to prefer THIRUVANANTHAPURAM to TRIVANDRUM.

KUMARAKOM

Kottayam

Peerumedu

Alappuzha

There are other similar places:
KOLLAM for Quilon;
ALAPPUZHA for Alleppey;
KOCHI for Cochin;
KODUNGALLUR for Crangannur;
KOZHIKODE for Calicut;
PALAKKAD for Palghat;
THALASSERRY for Tellicherry, and,
KANNUR for Cannanore
could be some of the confusing places for any visiting tourist.

Sabarimala

Chengannur

Pathanamthitta

Kayamkulam

Punalur

Shengotai

Kottarakkara

Kollam

Varkala

Nedumangadu

Legend

State Highways	
Railway Line (Broad Guage)	
Railway Line (Meter Guage)	
National Highway	

✈ **Trivandrum**

Kovalam

Nagercoil
Cape Comorin

*The borders shown on this map are neither authentic nor correct

Kerala

the land of blue lagoons and pearly beaches, emerald hills and green vales has an incomparable charm and elusive beauty. The ever changing scenario of tropical greenery, azure blue lagoons, traditional houses, shopping centres, restaurants and hotels make this land look like an ever expanding city with suburban tentacles. The myths and mythology of Kerala are vibrantly alive in her art forms, music and culture. The people of Kerala are famous for their literacy and development, for their enterprise and entrepreneurship.

A tourist visiting Kerala has lot of expectations. This land with its peculiar weather, greenery that arouses a feeling of disbelief and innumerable aspects of cultural differences and traditions gives a visitor many instances of exhilarating surprises.

Kerala has incomparable beauty as it has silvery beaches and azure blue lagoons. Its mountains have enormous variety of birds and animals. The myths and mythology vibrantly alive in the various art forms of Kerala present it as a land of ancient dreamy past and a land of promises for a bright future.

The entrepreneurship of Malayalis has been acknowledged abroad. Once Kerala's exports were limited to spices and sea food. Now they include manpower. Nurses in Western hospitals and technicians in the Cyber-countries have fully established the global presence of Malayalis.

The foreign tourists so long have been seduced by the Golden Triangle of Delhi, Jaipur and Agra of the Taj Mahal. One may not find any legacy of history enriched by battles or contests or any architectural heritage that withstood the upheavals of time in Kerala. Still the Travel and Leisure Magazine has featured Kerala as one of the 100 great trips of the 21st century and as one of the best breakfast destinations in the world.It is now identified as one of the 10 charming spots of the world. Kerala, widely known as God's own country has now become one of the fifty must - see destinations of the world, by the National Geographic Traveller.

Politically Kerala holds a unique record. It is the first state in the whole world where communists came to power through democratic means. During its recent history Kerala has been ruled alternatively by the Left Democratic Front and the Right United Democratic Front governments.

Kerala has a past that reveals a period of feudal supremacy, foreign invasions, protests, upheavals and social re-organization. It is a land where people faced social changes abruptly and accepted spiritualism and revolutionary ideologies with equal importance. A peep into its history would be an interesting experience.

According to a legend Kerala is believed to have risen from the sea at the behest of Lord Parasurama, the sixth incarnation of Vishnu who propitiated the God of the Seas, Varuna, to wrest land from the sea. But the pages of history tell us a different story. History tells us about the golden era of Kerala when KULASEKHARA PERUMAL ruled the country with excellent skills in administration. When we trace back the history further we find landmarks such as the period of rule of king BHANU VIKRAMA, the first King who established the supremacy of Brahmins and the reign of King Keralan who ruled the country for 12 years. It is believed that the state got its name from the King Keralan. Perhaps the land got its name "Kerala as it is the land of coconut palms.

KULASEKHARA PERUMAL who ruled Kerala for sometime brought about prosperity to the land. Hinduism

Kerala lives along the backwaters, throbbing with its own unique culture.

(Opposite page above)
Kerala's own live band

(Opposite page below)
Murals at Ettumanur Siva Temple. These exceptionally beautiful wall paintings depict mythological characters.

established a strong foothold during his tenure. Many of his successors came from outside the Kingdom.

It appears that the trading with Kerala, known as Malabar for most of its history, began in the 1st century BC. Greek and Roman traders first made the trips to Kerala via Africa, looking for its exotic spices. During this period, Jainism and Buddhism were the prominent religions in Kerala. But by the 3rd century BC, Hinduism had regained its strength. Even before the 3rd century BC, Egyptians, Phoenicians, Chinese and Babylonians had trade relations with Kerala.

Kerala came under the influence of Christianity when St. Thomas, the apostle landed at KODUNGALLOOR in AD 52. Many uppercast Hindus were converted to Christianity and they came to be known as Syrian Christians as St. Thomas came from Syria. Malik-Ibn-Dinar, disciple of Prophet Mohammed brought Islam to India. Incidentally the first mosque in the country was built in Kerala by Malik –Ibn-Dinar. He visited the country during AD 643.

After the disintegration of CHERA Empire, which ruled Kerala during AD 800 till AD 1102 the local Kings divided the state between them. They were the Zamorins of Calicut, the Raja of Cochin, the KOLATHIRIS of Cannanore and the King of Travancore. By the end of the 15th century, the Zamorin had half of Malabar under his rule.

SPLENDOUR OF THE SPICE LANDS

In the 15th century, when the monopoly of the spice trade became too expensive for the European markets to bear, Portugal financed Vasco da Gama to discover the sea route to the spice lands of Kerala. He landed at KAPPAD near Calicut in 1498. Vasco da Gama found a direct though lengthy route from Europe to India, by sailing round the Southern tip of Kerala. Vasco da Gama's journey was followed by a compatriot, Pedro Cabral, who was more commercially inclined than Gama.

However Cabral's demand to the Zamorin, the ruler of Calicut were extravagant and he had to leave Calicut. He found a better ally in the Raja of Cochin, who was looking for a prospective partner against his rival, the Zamorin.

TRADE RELATIONS WITH PORTUGUESE

The second visit of Vasco da Gama in 1502 was more aggressive. Arab merchant ships were sunk en route. The Portuguese were unsuccessful in making a trade agreement with the Zamorin because the Zamorin did not concede to the Portuguese demand of expelling the Malabar Muslims from the area. After a fierce attack on Calicut, the Portuguese moved to Cochin, where they were welcomed by the Raja of Cochin. In return to the gifts, the Cochin Raja granted exclusive trading agreement to the Portuguese. An infuriated Zamorin on hearing about the treaty attacked Cochin and established his garrison. But once the Zamorin returned to Calicut with his strike force, Portuguese squadron led by Albuquerque reinstated the Raja of Cochin. The Zamorin was defeated in 1509 by the Portuguese. The Portuguese supremacy on the Malabar thus established, remained unchallenged for 150 years. Later the Portuguese base was shifted to Goa. However their interest in India receded after Philip II of Spain incorporated their country into his domain. The Portuguese never won popularity in India.

Many interesting references about the trade relations

Chinese Fishing Nets
These huge nets erected between 1350 and 1450 AD by traders from the court of Kublai Khan are made of teak and bamboo. The cantilevered fishing nets are the best reminders of one of the first visitors to Fort Cochin.

of Kerala are available in the books written by eminent historians. Castanheda a Portuguese chronicler writes about a Gujarati pilot who led Vasco da Gama to Capacote and also refers to the ship belonging to the King of Gujarat loading the vessel at the port of Cannanore in 1501. The merchants from Malabar brought to this port arecanuts, coconuts, jaggery, cloves, cinnamon, mace, wax, emery, iron and sugar from Bhatkal, pepper, ginger, nutmeg, sandal wood, brazil wood, long pepper and silk from Malabar and China. These commodities were carried from Malabar ports to other countries. The Portuguese factory records during the period between 1525 and 1554 frequently mention Cambay opium as the most valued commodity at Malabar port. The trade existed between various pepper ports of Malabar and Coromandel continued in the sixteenth century. The vessels from Malabar carried spices, arecanuts, coconuts, and palm candy regularly to Coromandel and neighbouring ports in August and returned to Cochin in November or December. Passengers who were mainly merchants were also carried to and fro guarded by the Portuguese fleet patrolling the Arabian Sea. Merchant ships sailed along the entire coast taking not only spices from Malabar but also those products of the West such as leather, vermillion, coral, rose water and mercury.

Ottamthullal - This is a very popular form of classical performing arts of Kerala.

Since the beginning of the sixteenth century the Portuguese established direct commercial relationship with the ports on the Malabar coast. Casa da India (India House) was a department of trade and a customs house established in Lisbon in 1503. Dr. Manuel, the King of Portugal sent merchant ships every year to Malabar between 1500 and 1521. D. Jaoao III also showed keen interest in spice trade between Portugal and Malabar.

Among the Italian merchant financiers closely associated with the crown shipping in the oriental enterprise, Bertholomeo Marchioni occupied an important position. He sent a vessel to India in 1500 to purchase spices. His vessel carried spices from the Malabar coast. Girolamo Sernigi, a Florentine Merchant financier, settled in Lisbon, also sent a vessel to Malabar in 1500 in the fleet of Pedro Alvares Cabral. Giovani Francisco de Affaitati an influential banker in Portugal obtained permission from the King to participate in the direct trade with Malabar in 1502.

British mercantile companies established in British Cochin from 1850 onwards. Some of the leading companies were Peirce Leslie & Co., Aspinwall, Brinton, William Goodcare and Volkart Bros - a Swiss concern. These companies were located along the coast of the harbour mouth of Cochin.

Deity on the caparisoned elephant for a procession at Vadakkumnatha Temple, Thrissur.

THE DUTCH INFLUENCE

The Dutch formed an alliance with the Zamorin in 1604, with a view of expelling the Portuguese from Kerala. By 1663, the Dutch were in control of Cochin and Cannanore and had established a trading monopoly thanks to the KOLATHIRI.

Their dislike of the Roman Catholics was very open and all Catholic priests were expelled from their areas of control and Jesuit buildings demolished. However the Dutch were weakened by the wars with England and eventually they abandoned India, but not before returning to the Portuguese, with whom a rapproachement was reached, all their possessions in the Malabar coast, except Cochin. The Dutch were less corrupt and had better and fairer administration than the Portuguese. They had introduced advanced techniques in agriculture, salt farming and dyeing.

ARRIVAL OF THE ENGLISH

The first trading agreement between the East India Company and Zamorin of Calicut was made in 1625. This was in return to the help the English rendered to the Zamorin in expelling the Portuguese from Crangannore and Cochin. In 1662, the English made up with the Portuguese with the Royal wedding of Charles II to the Portuguese Princess of Braganza.

THE TRAVANCORE ROYALTY

The Kerala of 17th century lacked a central authority and the governance was degenerated by feudalism. The main rivalry was between the Zamorin of Calicut and the Raja of Cochin spanning over a period of 500 years. A brief period of Moghul rule in Kerala ended with the assassination of Aurangazeb, the last great Moghul. The Travancore royalty expanded its domain northward to the Periyar river during the rule of Raja Marthanda Varma (1729- '58). Many great developments were initiated including construction of waterways for transportation. The Raja then dedicated his kingdom to Lord Sree Padmanabha Swamy and became the 'servant' of the Lord. His successors also followed the system.

CONQUESTS AND BATTLES

The first Muslim invasion by Hyder Ali came from the adjoining state of Mysore. He was encouraged by Ali Raja of Cannanore to take over Kerala. Hyder Ali's supremacy was established in 1766 and Ali Raja was appointed governor of all conquests as a reward to his assistance to Hyder Ali. The English utilized the opportunity to help the Zamorin to get rid of Hyder Ali's forces. But the Muslims continued the fight till the English defeated Tipu Sultan, son and successor to Hyder Ali, and killed him in the battle of SRIRANGAPATNAM.

During the reign of Tipu, Kerala showed some improvement in the administrative system and technology. However, the economy took a nosedive since the trading came to a standstill. The gold and silver reserves disappeared, obviously to the Mysore coffers.

REVOLTS AND RESISTANCE

By 1793 Malabar was already in control of the East India Company. The administration was shifted from Bombay to Madras presidency in 1800. The English

Kanakakunnu Palace at Trivandrum - The palace and its sprawling grounds are today the venue for many cultural meets and programmes.

The Napier museum – a gem of an architectural exuberance, is combining traditional Kerala styles with good doses of Chinese and Mughal influences. The interior of the building designed by Chisholm, the 19th century English architect is truly intriguing. The pink and blue stripes alternating with stripes of yellow and chilly red, scalloped arches of banana yellow, elaborately carved balconies and the red mock friezes give us an impression of inimitable beauty and perfection. The collections in the museum can enlighten you about many things in history that have faded during the course of time. A curator can explain each and every detail of such collections.

gained control of the country in the early 19th century, by entering into trade agreements with the rulers of various territories on the pretext of providing protection and administrative assistance. In fact, the Rajas and their prime ministers did not enjoy any authority. All the major decisions were to be approved by the East India Company. The Company could effectively exploit the chaotic situation in the country, especially after the decline of Moghul empire. The Maharajas were satisfied with delegating the administration to the English, who they thought, could protect them from further invasions by the neighbours. The only resistance the East India Company faced was from Maharashrta.

Those who were willing to cooperate with the British administration had been treated with respect. Several incidents of revolts against the English occurred in different parts of Kerala. Prominent among them were the Paliyath Achan of Cochin, Raja of Kottayam, Veluthampi of Travancore and Kurichiyans of Wayanad. But their resistance was easily defeated since the English were better equipped and could mobilise more force to meet the challenge. By mid-19th century, barring Goa and Pondicherry, which were administered by the Portuguese (they continued till 1961), rest of India was controlled by the East India Company. Though the English rule was iron-handed, it gave birth to an industrial revolution and many technological advances. They had founded Universities at Bombay, Madras and Calcutta with an aim to create a middle class who could help the British in administration and remain loyal to British ideology. The British were far better than the Portuguese in religious matters. They never took interest in religious conversion, nor they interfered with the Hindus and Muslims. Social evils such as 'Sati' (self-immolation by a Hindu widow – prevalent in North India) and slavery were eradicated. But creating a middle class had an unexpected result. The educated Indian middle class founded Indian National Congress in 1855, which eventually turned into one big freedom movement.

PROTESTS

The freedom movement was strong in Kerala too. The 'Mappila Lahala' (revolt by the Muslims) in 1921 was one such incident of protests against British hegemony. Mahatma Gandhi's non-violent agitation soon gathered momentum and many campaigns were started against the British supremacy. Though India supported Britain in both the world wars, it was on the condition that India would be granted independence once the war was over .

Theyyam is a concept of Daivom meaning God,
And this ritual dance was evolved in the temples of
north Kerala.

DAWN OF FREEDOM

Arrangements were made to liberate India from the British rule in 1945. India was pronounced independent in August 1947. Tales of sincere struggle and sacrifices constituted the prelude to the independence. The present state of Kerala was established on 1st November 1956. Till then Malabar comprising of three states- Malabar, Cochin and Travancore- remained under the administration of Malabar.

Trivandrum was designated as the capital of the newly formed state of Kerala. In 1957 the first general elections were held and Kerala became the first state in India to give mandate for a communist government. The communists still have a strong presence in the state. The state is ruled alternatively by the left Democratic Front Governments led by the Communists and Congress partners. Coalition politics were put into practice and proved efficacious for the first time in Kerala.

ENCHANTING BEAUTY OF BACKWATERS

The backwaters of Kerala stretch over 1900 kms, providing drinking water and irrigating paddy fields. Backwaters refer to the large inland lakes of Kerala, consisting of the entire network of lakes, canals, estuaries and curious water formations.

The waterways of Kerala helped the state to develop its economy. Rice boats and small ships were used for carrying coconut, rubber, rice and spices to various trading centres of Kerala. Even today, these waterways link remote villages and islands with the main land. It is an incredibly different experience to cruise in the backwaters in country boats, closely observing the enticing beauty of Kerala villages.

A beautiful backwater spot, Kumarakom, slumbers by the Vembanad lake. The scenery flashes up vivid contrasts of breath - taking greens and deep blues. As the boat glides along, the gorgeous green of the fringed palms ripple in the blue waters and blend into silvery wavelets.

You can have an enthralling and intensive experience on the backwaters if you spend about nine hours to undertake a journey on a ferry boat from Quilon to Alleppey. But if you are less adventurous, there are short cruises arranged by private boat-owners in greater comfort. A cruise between Alleppey and Kottayam could be an unforgettable experience. You can also travel upto Cochin via these waterways. On a boat voyage to Alleppey through the Kuttanad, you can find yourself travelling along canals where the level of the water is often higher than that of the green fields on either sides.

Murikkan, a farmer, dearly referred as Krishi Raja, meaning King of farming had literally constructed Bunds around in almost 1800 acres of the lake and pumped out water to make it suitable for farming. Agriculture was the main occupation of people in Kerala in earlier times. However it has now become a losing proposition. A variety of cash crops are produced in Kerala that find a ready export market but the state depends on other states for its quota of rice. In subsequent years rubber displaced other crops, including paddy. The countryside is dotted with paddy fields and rubber groves providing a unique scene of intermingling shades of greenery.

The increasing prosperity of Kerala might soon deprive the backwaters of two familiar sights. The foot fishermen and the shell collectors.

Regular ferry and cargo boat traffic ply to and fro across the backwaters from dawn to dusk.

See the magic of nature. It happens on the same day – the morning and the evening.

It is often said that the children living on the banks of the backwaters learn to swim even before they learn to walk.

Today these backwaters act as vital waterways for the transport of goods, people and produce. They are often the only link between remote, isolated villages and crowded town pockets. As the night steps in, the dwellings on the small islands present a charming spectacle of lighted lamps or electric bulbs.

BOAT – RACES

Backwaters host many events during August – September. The electrifying races by carved wooden boats set the backwaters on fire. The 'Nehru Boat Race', named in honour of the late Prime Minister of India, Pandit Jawaharlal Nehru, is the most exciting of all the boat races. During the "ONAM" festival, many boat races, including the spectacular ARANMMULA boat –race, are conducted in the Alleppey region.

ARANMULA boat race linked to the VISHNU temple at ARANMULA, located on the banks of the Pampa river,

another sacred river. The boats of ARANMULA are legendary — graceful, with prows shaped like a bird, in homage to GARUDA — the vehicle of VISHNU(most gods in the Hindu pantheon have their own vehicles, like the bull of SIVA, the lion of PARVATHI the peacock of MURUGA or the rat of GANAPATHI). These dreams on the water can cleave the waves with an ease and felicity which is at once captivating and arresting. There are also the 130-feet-long, low-prowed snake-boats, with 20-feet-high sterns, which are permanent motifs at boat races in Kerala.

KUMARAKOM

Kumarakom is a favourite tourist hot spot in Kerala. A visitor can enjoy the beauty of the scenery, tranquillity in the surroundings and also enjoy the delicious dishes which include typical Kerala fish delicacies. A 14 acre bird sanctuary on the banks of the Vembanad lake, gives Kumarakom a unique place in the itinerary of a visitor. Waterducks, Cuckoos, Siberian Storks and many other migratory birds make Kumarakom a bird lover's paradise.

HOUSE BOATS

The traditional houseboat of Kerala is one of the most enduring images of the backwaters.

These houseboats are converted versions of the "KUTTANADAN KETTUVALLAMS", comfortably furnished and offer adequate accommodation for a whole family, with a sitting room, a bedroom and a kitchen. One can create one's own world of imagination and enjoy the beauty of the surroundings while travelling in a houseboat.

The country boats were designed to carry cargo, such as coconut and spices, and to provide living accommodation for the boatmen.

The history of Kerala's backwaters is inextricably bound to the "Kettuvallom" (House Boats) the transportation needs of people and trade over the years. Although these boats were used to carry coconut and spices from coast to coast, older families of Kuttanad used them on family outings.

A few of them offer holidayers the ultimate backwater experience.

Preserving their historic character and style, our craftsmen have created a unique atmosphere. Tourists book KETTUVALLOMS for a week or so, stopping en route to discover a village, pay a visit to a church or temple. There are tours which take one from Cochin to Alleppey or Quilon. Such tours are also available in North Kerala.

On board, is a luxurious, self contained world from which one can observe rural Indian life flowing gently by. Whether it's an exploratory, overnight cruise through narrow canals; a gentle circumnavigation around the still, vast water of Lake Vembanad, or a longer passage from Cochin to Alleppey, the experience will be quite different from any other holiday. Something that will linger on as an everlasting memory in the mind of a tourist.

One couple has the exclusive run of the entire boat ensuring privacy for honeymooners- and guests are attended to by a personal cook and two boatmen. There is a cosy double bedroom midships, with an en suite bathroom, and a beautifully furnished sitting room complete with its own sun deck at the bow. In the stern, there is a fully equipped kitchen with all kinds of modern amenities. Ever mindful of the environment, power is supplied by discreet solar panels hidden on the roof, and the boat, almost 50 feet long, is propelled from the bow and stern by the two boatmen using punting poles. (An outboard motor is sometimes used on longer cruises)

A Chinese influence can be seen in the design of Kettuvallom - the slides open up to create winged awnings, giving shade but also an unobstructed view of the passing scenery. For the boatmen, the Kettuvallom is second home. They sleep, cook and eat on it. The Kettuvallom is the genesis of a cuisine, songs and stories that revolve around the backwaters and the boat.

CAPTIVATING BEACHES

Beaches in Kerala are places which present serenity of nature in its true perspective. If one loves the vastness of the sea that touches the distant horizon and enjoys the music of frothy waves that beat on the shores, beaches are ideal places for leisure time meditation as well as merriment. KOVALAM beach 14 kms from Trivandrum is an ideal place for rest and recreation. Rocky headlands separate the lighthouse Beach and Hawah Beach. Well known guest houses and restaurants behind the beach provide all comforts including excellent sea food to the tourists. KOVALAM's fishermen can be seen at dawn returning to VIZHINJAM in the powered vessels and in the traditional country boats.

Varkala beach is considered to be a holy beach. It is also known as PAPANASHINI, Keralites from deferent parts of the world come here to pray for their ancestors.

Marari beach near ALAPPUZHA is a gentle stopping beach favoured by both domestic and foreign tourists. The beach at CHERAI, off VYPEEN near Ernakulam, offers both rural and urban ambience. NATTIKA near Thrissur offers beach-games and relaxation.

The Bekal Tourist Resort developed by the Kerala Tourism Department, is a halcyon place. The tourists can explore the unrivalled solitude in KAPPAD beach, the MUZHUPPILANGADI beach, PAYYAMBALAM beach and ANJARAKANDY beach. Kerala offers a unique experience to all tourists who visit such beaches. Perhaps nowhere in the world one can enjoy such close proximity with the sea in a marvellous ambience.

Quite unusual-a tusker enjoying the sunbath

A barber on the move-people need not go to the beauty parlour

The Fisherman and the sea

Childhood innocence

The waves make their job very easy.

Baskets are ready to carry home the marine wealth.

Safety check – before the take-off

Sea-food is a hot favourite of the Keralites.

The fishermen in groups brave the sea in their small and large boats for the daily catch.

" I am not ashamed to pose for the camera"

KALAMEZHUTHU

KALAMEZHUTHU is unique form of art found only in Kerala. Here it is essentially a temple art. The patterns to be drawn and the colours chosen are traditionally stipulated, and the tradition is strictly adhered to.

KALAMS are drawn in connection with the worship of DEVI, NAGA and SASTHA. It is typically Indian as it is a harmonic blend of Arian, Dravidian and Tribal traditions.

The drawing is done directly with the hand, that is, without using any tools whatsoever. The powders used are all natural (Vegetable or Mineral or combined).

Usually KALAMEZHUTHU is conducted as part of the general festivities in the temple, or as part of a major ritual like NAGAPUJA. Offerings like rice and other grains are heaped in certain places in and around the drawing and the room is decorated with flowers, leaves and garlands.

Kalams (drawings on the floor) are rubbed out soon after the rituals.

MUDIYETTU

MUDIYETTU depicts the fight between KALI and DARIKA. It begins with KALAMAZHIKKAL (Wiping out of the floor painting) MUDIYETTU literally means wearing the crown on the head. Once the person representing KALI in the ritual wears the headgear, he gets possessed by a certain spiritual force. And throughout the night he remains possessed till the battle ends with the killing of DARIKA. KALI is accompanied by her attendant spirits and KOIMPIDAR (a character representing the virtuous in society) the side of DARIKA is DANAVA to help him fight against Kali. The battle scenes are enacted with dramatic realism.

PADAYANI

PADAYANI is a very colourful and enchanting folk form associated with the festivals of a few temples in the southern parts of Kerala.

The word PADAYANI means rows of army and the performance is a symbolic victory march of Goddess KALI after eliminating DARIKA the demon. The performers present a dance procession, ending at the altar of the deity. The performers impersonating as KOLAMS will have huge headgears with projections and a mask for the face. There is no time limit for this performance.

The Padayani masks are made of leaf sheaths of arecanut trees on which drawings of gods and godesses are made with natural colours.

PLACES OF WORSHIP

The temples of Kerala reflect the architectural beauty typical to this state. These ancient temples occupy a large area of space. You have to walk through courtyards-within – courtyards before reaching the sanctum-sanctorum. The walls of the temples are covered with carvings and motifs. Many scenes from the epics RAMAYANA and MAHABHARATA are depicted in murals. SIVA THANDAVA is a famous mural motif. PADMANABHA PURAM palace and VADAKUMNATHA Temple as well as the ETTUMANOOR Temple and TRIPRAYER have enchanting panels of RAMAYANA characters. Murals reveal a world of fantasy and imagination. Many Kerala temples have murals dating back to the 16th and 17th century. PADMANABHA PURAM PALACE has murals over 900 sq. feet depicting such scenes of valour and mythological events of importance that can compel a visitor to observe them with curiosity. PADMANABHA PURAM palace is called the Mural Pagoda of Kerala. It is believed that the first treatise on murals called 'SILPARATNAM' was written by Sreekumaran in 16th century. The colours for murals are prepared from, paste made out of juices of plants, paste made out of leaves of certain trees, lamp soot etc., The ancient inscriptions on murals are available in temples at TIRUNANTHAKKARA, KANTHALLOOR, THRIVIKRAMANGALAM, PARTHOVAPURAM, and CHITHARAL CAVE temple. The murals seen in Kerala were created during the 15th century. The SABARIMALA Temple in the high ranges is visited by pilgrims from all castes and communities hailing from all parts of India. The SASTHA or AYYAPPA cult is growing phenomenon now, extending to other states in India. The pilgrim season is consisted of the 41 day MANDALAVILAKKU and 14 day MAKARAVILAKKU. "THANKA ANKI" procession is conducted during the MANDALAPOOJA from ARANMULA to SABARIMALA.

The BHADRAKALI temples at KODUNGALLOOR and CHOTTANIKKARA still preserve certain hoary traditions. In CHOTTANIKKARA the first shrine is located at a higher place. At the bottom of a great stairway near a pond is the second shrine where some special rituals are held to exorcise evil spirits. Some people believe that evil spirits get inside the bodies of weak minded people. In the inner compound stands a tree punctured by hundreds of long steel nails.

The possessed patients hammer nails into the bark of the tree with their heads to clamp the spirits to the Godess BHADRAKALI. The possessed person does this in a state of trance. Every night the goddess is fed her supper-twelve basins of blood-coloured solution, made by mixing juice of tender coconuts, turmeric and lime. At this time the Goddess makes the devils dance. The possessed women and girls shake their heads, put the long hair backward and forward and present a series of convulsions. Some of them turn around like a top and scream and shriek aloud. At the KODUNGALLOOR temple offering of cocks for sacrifice and 'KAVUTHEENDAL' of VELICHAPPADUS are some rituals that receive publicity every year.

SPIRITUAL LIBERATION

Sankaracharya was the proponent of ADVAITA philosophy. He was born in Kalady on April 3, 509 B C. The above mentioned date of the birthday of the philosopher and GURU has been accepted unanimously by Sankaracharyas across the country who control the 'MATHS' established by Adi Sankara. Sankaracharya revived Hindu religion. His ADVAITA philosophy stresses the presence of God within you and describes life as an illusion. Perhaps he was the first sage who liberated Hinduism from the stranglehold of Buddhism.

When Sree Narayana Guru preached that there was only one God, and what was needed was the improvement of man, whatever be his religion, the curse of untouchability was ravaging the social fabric of Kerala. He elevated

Qutheeb-the person who leads the NAMAZ *(Muslim's Prayer)*

Below: A Hindu priest (Pujari) does the routine religious rites at the temple.

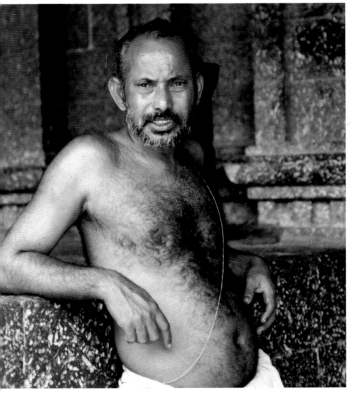

EZHAVAS psychologically and socially by erecting separate temples for them to worship in defiance of upper castes NAMBUDIRIS. Sree Narayana Guru established an ASHRAM in VARKALA. His SAMADHI or last resting place is at VARKALA and it has become a famous pilgrimage centre. The place has also acquired sanctity as Hindus reach here to offer last rites for the dear departed at the PAPANASAM area of the beach. The Janardana Swamy Temple at VARKALA is another landmark of the place.

CHURCHES

Kerala had Christians as long as Christianity has been in Europe. The Portuguese were more than surprised to find Christianity already established along the Malabar coast when they arrived here centuries ago. The Christian Community played a vital role in the trade and commerce of the state. Christianity in Kerala now follows different rites having the Catholics, the orthodox Church with headquarters in Antioch, the Chaldeans, the Jacobites, the Mar Thomites, the Canonites, the Pentecostal church, the Church of the God, the Seventh Day Adventists, the Yehovah's witnesses and various other minor sects, with their own individual churches.

The early churches had a similarity with the temples in the architecture. Various elements such as the impressive gateways or an open-air cross in front of the building are borrowings from the temple-tradition. This form of architecture underwent a change when the Portuguese introduced the Roman form of architecture. Later, renovations brought in further changes and many new churches are now built in contemporary style.

The St.Mary's Church Bharananganam near Palai – the place where the mortal remains of sister Alphonsa (1916-1946) was interned in a chapel next to the St.Mary"s Church. This 1000-year-old church features an attractive Grotto of Virgin Mary.

St.Francis Church. Considered India 's oldest Church. Vasco da Gama who died in Cochin in 1524 was buried here before his remains were returned to Portugal 14 years later.

The Cheria Palli, Kottayam – Built in 1579 A.D. Yet stronger than most modern structures. It has some murals and paintings depicting Biblical and other themes.

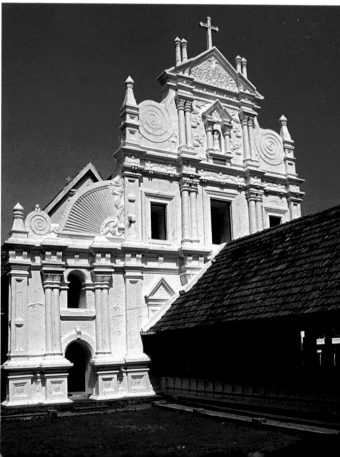

SNAKE WORSHIP

Since ancient days snake worship prevailed in Kerala. Almost every house has SARPA KAVUS (Sacred groves) in compounds where snake dieties were worshipped with special rituals. In many parts of Kerala still people worship snake deities. The Brahmin priest who performs the special rituals pours a paste of turmeric powder mixed with juice of tender coconuts in small bowls made of leaves. Lighted wicks and small torches of fire are kept in front of the snake dieties. In an elaborate ritual called SARPABALI the snake gods are propitiated by special rituals. The Brahmin priest makes big balls of turmeric powder and with the chanting of mantras place lighted wicks on the balls. The chanting of mantras and the rituals continue for hours together. The temple at MANNARSALA near Alleppey,the temple PAMPUMMEKAVU near Trichur and at AMEDA near Tripunithura are dedicated to the snake gods.

A special ritual called SARPAM THULLAL is performed to propitiate the Snake-gods. When a PULLUVAN, and his associate sing a devotional song to the accompaniment of a primitive string instrument, a couple of devotees get possessed by the spirits of the deities start a devotional dance. Those who are possessed by the spirits of deities do the devotional dance by twists and turns and sometimes crawl on the floor or wriggle their bodies like snakes. Usually young girls or women do such devotional dance and they rub out the drawing or KALAM before they fall unconscious after finishing their dance. Most of the temples in Kerala have special places allotted only for the worship of snake deities. Snake worship in Kerala if traced back could be seen associated with the custom of worshipping animals and birds and natural forces prevalent in ancient days when Aryans reached India with their characteristic culture, traditions and beliefs.

KALAMS or floor drawings depicting NAGAS or Snake gods are drawn with rice powder, turmeric, lime and burned husk of paddy.

The Odathil Palli is two hundred years old. Curiously Odathil is but a modification for the Portuguese word for garden.

MOSQUES

Malik-Ibn-Dinar landed at Crangannore (KODUNGALLOOR) in the eighth century and his faith Islam found its way to Kerala. Later, many Arab traders travelled to Malabar and quite few had settled there.

The mosques are usually in the form of a covered structure with a large prayer hall in the centre. They also employ arches associated with the Islamic tradition. Superbly carved wooden pulpits are real pieces of art.

SYNAGOGUES

Kerala had a community of Jews from very early times. The many privileges granted to the Jewish community by the then King BHASKARA RAVIVARMAN were recorded on a copper plate and preserved in the Jewish Synagogue at Mattancherry, Cochin. The Synagogue, built in AD 1568 is the most important Jewish monument. The interior is one of the finest of any synagogue in the world, beautifully decorated with Chinese hand-painted blue and white tiles differing slightly in design. The mid 18th century floor tiles were brought from Canton by Ezekial Rababi as part of his reconstruction work. The crystal chandeliers were made in Belgium in the 19th century. The golden crowns were presented by the MAHARAJAS of Cochin and Travancore. Remnants of Buddhists and Jain temples can also be seen along the state.

The Jewish Synagogue, Mattancherry, boasts of several finely wrought gold and silver crowns gifted to the synagogue.

A Residence at Fort Cochin with tiled roofs and timber architecture of Dutch design.

TRADITIONAL ARCHITECTURE

Kerala has a rich legacy of architectural excellence. The ancient buildings, temples and monuments reflect the styles of sculpture and wood works adopted by artisans from different sources. One can easily identify the influence of Chinese, Persian and European styles of architecture in certain buildings in Kerala. Various carvings on wood reveal the regal splendour that was once confined only to the palaces and courts of eminent kings or regents.

A typical MALABAR house has a distinct aura about it. A luxuriant garden with jackfruit tree, coconut and arecanut palms and the broad – leaved banana plants, is an integral part of the household. A visit to such a house would arouse nostalgic memories of an aristocracy that dominated in the early period of Kerala's history.

Traditional Kerala house has a distinct style referred to as NALUKETTU (four sided) and ETTUKETTU (eight sided) based on a modular concept that allows the house to grow in geometrical progression. The four wings of a NALUKETTU house are built around an open courtyard with or without a covered VARANDHA on all four sides. The courtyard allows air and light to circulate and also provides for the rain.

The architectural beauty of traditional Kerala village can be enjoyed at Kumarakom, where history of 70 -150 years has been recreated by skilled craftsmen.

A famous Hotel group has recreated the Kerala Village at Kumarakom. Old Wooden houses have been carefully transplanted from various villages, piece by piece by efficient craftsmen. The houses have been rebuilt in its original form.

VOC Gate- built in 1740 this wooden gate facing the Parade Ground has the monogram (VOC) of the Dutch East India Company.

NATURAL RICHES

Kerala has been famous from time immemorial for its natural riches of Grand teaks, rosewood, ebony, sandalwood and an assortment of fruit – bearing trees. Tucked in the mountains are small hill-stations, plantations and wild – life sanctuaries.

The high ranges of Kerala is exotic with the spice plantations. Cardamom, black pepper, cinnamon and ginger grow in abundance. Moving higher, the mesmerizing greens of the tea estates and coffee plantations will enthral you. The winding roads take you along the rubber plantations and small, friendly towns, where you can stop for a while for a cup of steaming tea or coffee. The life you see in the high ranges has a uniqueness about it.

Munnar is still very much a British tea plantation town, tea gardens carpet entire hillsides. Nimble-fingered women are engaged in plucking the daily crop of "two leaves and bud" every morning.

SPICES PLANTATIONS

Kerala was known for its spices and travellers from around the world journeyed here to trade and to gain control over this rich land. The first travellers were the Greeks, the Romans the Arabs and the Chinese.

Later-day traders included the Portuguese, the Dutch, The French and the British. It is believed that the spice trade dates back three thousand years. Certainly it was responsible for Vasco da Gama's quest for the Indian subcontinent, and his discovery via a sea route. Pepper still remains the king of Kerala's spices, but the state also has a very rich produce in cardamom, cinnamon, nutmeg, mace, ginger and turmeric; it has a rich cultivation of cashewnuts, and is India's home state for coconut.

As in the past, the state continues to be spice capital of the world. Visitors to Kerala, especially the tourists,

Coffee beans

prefer to see for themselves how the different spices are grown, harvested, processed and packed.

Kerala's climate and geography make it ideal for the cultivation of coffee, tea, cardamom, pepper, coconut, paddy and rubber.

SPICE WEALTH

IDUKKI provides a marvellous scene of pepper wines entwined on trees and cardamom plants heavy with cardamom seeds. The spices are auctioned at KUMILY in THEKKADY. The bio-diversity displayed by a large variety of spices in the hills around THEKKADY is something worth noticeable. Precious spices like the nutmeg, cinnamon, cloves and vanilla enrich the hills with the spice wealth. The cashewnut trees, pineapple and tapioca plants comprise the vast stretches of green orchards spread over the hills. Tapioca has now become a staple food of Kerala farmers. It is believed that tapioca was brought to Kerala by the Portuguese. Nowadays even in big restaurants tapioca is served in delicious preparations. Tapioca in combination with fish curry is regarded as a gourmet's delight.

WILDLIFE SANCTUARIES

Kerala boasts of more than a dozen wild life sanctuaries filled with Indian elephants, wild boars, tigers, lion-tailed monkeys, ibex and leopards.

The Periyar wildlife sanctuary is one of the major wild life sanctuaries in India. A boat – cruise in the Periyar lake can elevate you to ecstasy. You can watch elephants in their natural habitat from the boat you are travelling in. There are at least 160 species of birds in this sanctuary. Apart from the Great Indian Hornbill one could spot Brahminy Kite, Blackwinged kite, little Cormorant, Pied kingfisher, Golden Oriole and Hawk cuckoo.

Set amidst dense and evergreen forests, marshes and valleys, is PARAMBIKULAM Sanctuary which is home to the bisons. Unlike Periyar, PARAMBIKULAM have fewer facilities, with the emphasis on preserving the natural environment.

The ERAVIKULAM National Park is a mere 30-minutes drive from the tea-town of MUNNAR. Home to thousands of Ibex, this is a spot of endless and rare beauty.

The Periyar Wildlife Sanctuary- beautiful birds such as Malabar Hornbill, Grey heron, jungle fowl and jungle mynah live in the sanctuary. 266 species of birds have been positively recorded.

The Eravikulam Wildlife Sanctuary- the natural habitat of the Nilgiri Tahr. Half the world population of the rare mountain goat (Hemitragas hylocres), which is fast becoming extinct, is now found here. The Nilgiri Tahrs are today reduced to small herds found in the Eravikulam – Rajamala region.

Gaur – these are shy but ferocious looking bovines perhaps the largest in the world. Gaurs are popularly known as Indian bison. The male bison weighs over 900 kgs, grows up to 6 feet in height and are black skinned. Female gaurs are smaller in size and the colour of their skin is brownish black.

*Periyar wildlife sanctuary is the home ground for bisons,
antelopes, sambar, wild boar, monkeys, langur, herds of
elephants (approx. 800), around 41 tigers and a variety of
birds and butterflies.*

NEYYAR wild life sanctuary stretching from NEYYATINKARA
taluk to MUNDANTHURAI Tiger Reserve in Tamil Nadu,
was established in 1958. It has a crocodile farm and a
lion safari park. One can see elephants, gaurs, sambars,
barking deer, wild boars, lion-tailed macaques etc. in
natural surroundings and also birds such as kingfishers,
white breasted water hens, little egrets, brahminy kites
etc. in this sanctuary.

Peppara wild life sanctuary is 50 km northeast of
Thiruvananthapuram city. Animals like gaurs, sambars,
wild boars etc. and birds like little cormorants, pied

kingfishers etc, can be seen in beautiful surroundings.

SHENDURUNY wildlife sanctuary is in PATHANAPURAM taluk 66km from Kollam town. The sanctuary has west coast tropical evergreen forest and animals like lion-tailed macaque, Nilgiri langur, bonnet macaque etc. make it an ideal place of eco-tourism.

CHINNAR wildlife sanctuary occupies the forested region on other side of the MARAYOOR-UDUMALPET road. One can watch the fascinating wildlife comprised of panthers, sambars, Hanuman langurs, the endangered grant grizzled squirrels etc. A couple of good trekking trails make it an ideal place for adventures.

THATTEKKAD bird sanctuary occupies the catchment area of the BHOOTHATHANKETTU Dam. It has rare birds like

crimson-throated barbets, bee-eaters, sunbirds, fairy blue birds grey-headed fishing eagles etc.

CHIMMINI wildlife sanctuary lies in the western valley of NELLIAMPATHY in the MUKUNDAPURAM taluk of Thrissur district Wild bisons, leopards, elephants, wild pigs etc. present a good scenario of variety in wild life.

ARALAM wildlife sanctuary is situated next to the Central State Farm at ARALAM in Kannur district. Mainly teak and eucalyptus plantations comprise the vegetation of this area.

ECO-DELIGHTS

The Silent Valley is a unique preserve of tropical rain forests. It locates the SAIRANDHRI VANAM and River KUNTHI gives a mythological back-drop to the National park. This part of the Malabar rain forests harbours about 1000 species of plants, including 966 species of flowering plants belonging to 134 families. It has an exotic variety

Soft and hard treks with professional guides - the Periyar wildlife sanctuary.

of beautiful orchids and a fair representation of mammals and rare species of birds.

VYTHRI provides ideal base for wild life tourism. It is treated in Wayanad in North Kerala. The Eco-tourists consider Wayanad as the latest breakway because of the tree houses atop the tall ficus resembles the ERUMADAM of the tribals, it offers all modern amenities, including Eco-friendly food, power and light.

One can savour the incomparable view of mountains, tea plantations and misty mountains affording endless opportunities to stroll or track from PONMUDI near Trivandrum. It also offers a variety of orchids and other botanical rarities.

MUNNAR is a unique hill station situated amidst a vast undulating green vista of tea bushes. It has many a colonial relic which can be savoured by the nostalgic foreigner. There are 14 peaks in Idukki district with an average altitude of 2000 feet for those interested in climbing, peninsular India's highest peak, the ANAMUDI is situated in Munnar, four and a half hour's drive from THEKKADY. RAMAKKALMEDU is another point gaining in popularity, with facilities for wind surfing and sky-diving Munnar has the High Range Club with its colonial ambience, bison-head-studded walls and a display of hats of past members- and a beautiful golf course.

Bamboo rafting in lake Periyar enables you to get close
to the wild animals.

Don't I look stylish?

COOL CLIMATE

The PERIYAR wild life sanctuary covers 777 square kilometres of the Western Ghats. The PERIYAR lake is a vast reservoir of dammed water on the PERIYAR River; constructed in 1895 by then Governor of Madras, Lord Venlock, for irrigation. As early as 1899, the forests around the lake were declared as reserve forests. With an annual rainfall of 2500 mm every year from May to July and an altitude varying from 3000 to 6700 feet, THEKKADY is cool in summer (22 degrees ,to 30 degrees). Its pleasant climate attracted the erstwhile royalty of TRAVANCORE to construct a palace in the heart of the forest to escape from the severe summer heat.

THE PERIYAR WILD LIFE SANCTUARY

The Lake is an important source of water for the many wild animals. The best time to visit PERIYAR is between October and May. The best chance of watching animals is during the hot months of March, April and May, when water gets low and the grass dries out and animals especially of March, April and May, when water gets low and the grass dries out and animals especially elephants come down to the PERIYAR lake to bathe and frolic in the waters along with their young ones. The PERIYAR wild life sanctuary at THEKKADY in IDUKKI district is 253 km from Trivandrum and 192 km from Cochin. The Forest Department has a watchtower at PERIYAR, which can be reached by boat from THEKKADY.

Here green, gold and blue merge to create a splendid scene of beauty. This is the interior of the Periyar forest reserve, the sanctuary which nurtures tigers, elephants, and a host of other birds and animals. The Periyar lake is sandwiched by the forest and boating in the lake offers a glimpse of the interior of the forest, the habitat of these wild animals, where they play, bathe, feed, mate and proliferate.

TIGER

The tiger is the chief predator in the Indian jungles save the Gir in Gujarat where the Asiatic lion, in its last home, reigns supreme. The tiger has 6 to 7 sub-species, the Siberian tiger being the largest, sometimes measuring up to almost 4m. in length. The Indian tiger is also a large animal averaging a little less than 3 m. length. This great cat is a solitary animal except when tigers are courting or when a tigress is with her cubs

which only have their mother after reaching maturity at the age about 2 years. Tigers hunt on the large herbivores including chital, sambar and other deer, gaur, wild boar etc. No one can ever forget the first sighting of this great cat in the wild. Even a brief glance is an unforgettable experience. But it is a shy and alert animal, hence difficult to see and observe at ease.

ELEPHANTS

Elephants live in herds with a leader which is often an old and experienced cow. A herd also has master bull which dominates other bulls. Not all bull elephants have tusks and those without are called MAKHNAS. Cow elephants in India, unlike in Africa, do not have tusks. This enormous animal is the largest of the land mammals.

An elephant requires ten to fifteen hours of grazing everyday to keep it going. It feeds on grass, tree barks and so on. The elephant is a very intelligent animal, has a highly developed sense of smell and hearing but its eyesight is poor. Its young are sometimes attacked by tigers, but this is very rare as the herd defends the young extremely efficiently and even ferociously. Man, of course, has hunted this great animal for ivory for hundreds of years, but today the elephant, found in many forests in India, is a protected animal.The Indian elephant is generally found in the Western Ghats, Orissa, Bihar, UP and West Bengal. The gestation period of an elephant is about 20-22 months. The new born

weighs approximately 100 kgs and stands 90 cm tall. The protection of the baby-elephant is the responsibility of females in the group. Apart from the mother, the young ones are suckled by other females. The baby-elephant observes the elders to learn all aspects of elephant life. The suckling continues till the age of 2 years, but may continue for a longer period in the wild. For the first few years babies, male and female, grow at the same rate. Thereafter the male elephant outgrows the female. But while the life-expectancy of the male elephants is generally 50 years, the female lives longer, say 60 years.

THE WORLD OF COLOURS AND DREAMS

Kerala presents such scenic beauty that a mere stroke of a brush of an artist brings out splendid reflection of the surroundings which are his perpetual source of inspiration. Kerala always enjoyed supremacy in the field of painting and sculptures in ancient days. Raja Ravi Verma, one of the earliest painters commanded technical mastery. He is considered to be a pioneer in oil paintings that adopted Western academic style. He was an expert in portrait paintings. The contemporary artists in Kerala produce excellent works of artistic perfection and reflect the influences of modern trends in paintings. The intricacies of human mind and the impact of the drastic changes on the society due to rapid industrialisation or urbanisation frequently become powerful themes for self expression for eminent artists. One can find a harmonious blend of classic and modern styles in the works of such artists.

MURALS

Temples are also the treasure houses of art forms like murals, a typical Kerala art form. Mural paintings are visual manifestations of the legends of gods and deities and demons. Popular among them are RAMA, KRISHNA, BHIMA, HANUMAN and NARASIMHAM. PURANIC episodes of SIVA and VISHNU are depicted in these murals. SIVA THANDAVA is also a famous mural motif. PADMANABHA PURAM PALACE, and VADAKKUNNATHA Temple as well as the ETTUMANUR temple and TRIPRAYAR have magnificent panels of RAMAYANA characters. Many Kerala temples have murals dating back to the 16th and 17th century. Mural characters resemble KATHAKALI figures, again, depicting the RAMAYANA and the MAHABHARATHA characters.

KATHAKALI

KATHAKALI is the most famous dance-drama of Kerala. This classical art form is distinguished by several unique features. It is a marvellous blend of the TANDAVA (masculine) and LASYA (exotic) elements of dancing. It is believed that KATHAKALI originated from RAMANATTOM, a temple art popularized by KOTTARAKKARA THAMPURAN.

The origin of KATHAKALI is considered to be more than 1500 years old. The costume, make-up, movements and expressions make KATHAKALI a treat. The actors do not speak, but enact the PADAMS (dialogues) sung by the singers behind. The themes of KATHAKALI are drawn from Indian myth and the characters are gods and demons. The stories revolve around the lives, loves and times of gods and demons.

KATHAKALI consists of three fine arts, ABHINAYAM (acting) NRITYAM (dancing) and GEETAM (singing). The actors enact their roles with the help of MUDRAS (hand-gestures) and facial expressions.

Music is a very essential aspect of KATHAKALI. If reflects the emotions and feelings of the characters in a story.

Two musicians sing the PADAMS. Drums-CHENDA and MADDALAM provide the percussion. The music, though carnatic, has a typical flavour of Kerala and it adheres to the THALA (rhythm) instead of RAAGA.

The costumes of KATHAKALI are designed for the various mythological characters presented. The splendour of the costumes, ornaments, and facial make-up transform the actor dancer into a type a rather than a particular character. There are five major types of costume designs, each having set modes of make up, attire and adornment. Each type denotes certain characteristics or qualities possessed by the character. These types are usually known by the predominant colour applied to the face or its pattern. They are PACHA (green) KATHI (Knife) THAADI (beard) KARI (Black) and MINUKKU (Polished).

PACHA denotes virtuous and noble characters. The KATHI type includes the proud, aggressive and unrighteous characters. THAADI or the bearded type are of three varieties- CHUVANNA THAADI (red beard) denotes the aggressive and demoniac; VELLATHAADI (White beard) denotes mythical and fabulous beings like the Monkey-Gods and KARUTHA THAADI (black beard), the tribesmen and forest-men. The KARI type represents low characters. The MINUKKU type women, sages, Brahmins etc., whose appearance has polished look.

KATHAKALI is presented at night, for festivals it runs whole night till dawn.

The Vijnana Kala Vedi centre is situated in Aranmula on the bank of the sacred river Pamba.

Louba Schild, French scholar of the Indian Government through the Indo-French Cultural exchange programme studied and performed kathakali since 1969 in Kerala. The wish to share her rich experience with other westerners inspired her to organise courses offering the study of traditional arts and crafts of Kerala. In 1977, Louba Schild created the Vijnana Kala Vedi.

Vedi is the 'sacred stage' where Vijnana 'Knowledge' and Kala 'art' are to be displayed.

The centre organizes courses in theatre, dance, music, painting, wood carving, martial art, cooking etc, in their natural environment. Student can stay for any long and learn these arts or languages. Accommodation and food is provided and the lessons are mostly individual in nature. Detailed information can be had from their web site, www.vijnanakalavedi.org

THEYYAM

This is a ritual dance form, and one of Kerala's finest artistic expressions of a glorious past. THEYYAM is associated with cult of Goddess BHAGAWATI. The themes of these dances revolve around the triumph of the Goddess over the evil characters like the demon DARAKA (DARAKASURAN). THEYYAM is always performed by men and they are often dressed up as women in exotic make-up. The men performing the dance wear masks and elaborate costumes. The head-dress made of palm leaves and cloth can at times rise well over forty feet in height! The dancer moves to the rhythm of CHENDA (drum) and when the dance picks up momentum, he casts a spell on the spectators, often in a religious way.

KOODIYATTAM

The Aryans, who came to this land centuries before the beginning of the Christian era, brought with them the language Sanskrit and also certain customs and traditions. They introduced a new dance form, KOODIYATTAM, which unlike the most other dance forms, include women participants. Since KOODIYATTAM performances were regarded as offering to the deity, they were enacted only in temples. For the purpose, many temples have beautiful pavilions within their precincts which are known as KOOTHAMBALAMS, with high sloping roofs covered with metal sheets.

A KOODIYATTAM performance is a long drawn- out affair, taking place at night and lasting for days. The story unfolds in a leisurely manner and the text is augmented by the performers by expanding upon them with anecdoted, satire and innuendos. Politics, philosophy and social behaviour are covered in the comments. The pivotal role in these performances belong to the Jester VIDOOSHAKAN or SOOTHRADHARAN, as he is the only one who speaks Malayalam the language of the ordinary people. He translates the Sanskrit version with a touch of humour. He also acts as an interpreter between the actor and the audience.

MOHINIYATTOM

It is the typical dance form of Kerala that exudes enchantment, grace and passion. MOHINIYATTAM is a fusion of BHARATANATYAM and dynamism and vigour of KATHAKALI. The performances are done only by women. MOHINIYATTAM has several phases in its presentation such as SOLKETTU, VARNAM, PADAM, THILLANA, KAIKOTTIKKALI, KUMMI and SWARAM. The predominant mood created is SRINGARAM (erotic).

Mohiniyattom-the Dance of the enchantress is far more culture-bridging, because it depicts emotions in ways which are universally understood.

The performing artist is dressed in traditional costumes consisting of MUNDU and MELMUNDU (Dhoti with Jarikar border worn around abdomen and chest, the second one on top of the other) Hairstyle is traditional, hair bunched together at the side of the head and adorned by white flowers. In MOHINIYATTAM, the LASYA element dancing is predominant, and the mood created is SRINGARAM (erotic) MOHINIYATTAM literally means the 'Dance of the Temptress'. All performing arts in Kerala have a ritualistic background. Preparation for each form is a ritual as well, which include fasting and special diet. PAVAKOOTHU, MUDIYETTU, PADAYANI, KAKKARISSI NATAKAM, THIRUVATHIRAKALI and KUMMATTIKALI, PAWAKOOTHUKALI are some of the other folk dance forms. THIRUVATHIRAKALI involves simple rhythmic steps and is performed by women focussed on getting good husbands by propitiating the goddess PARVATHI. On the auspicious day of THIRUVATHIRA women observe fasting, wear ten kinds of flowers called DASAPUSHPAM and take a dip in rivers or ponds and sing devotional songs praising Goddess PARVATHI.

OTTAMTHULLAL

This is a very popular form of classical performing arts of Kerala. The actor wears a long tape of cloth, looped around a waist-string to form a knee-length skirt. A chest-plate adorned by coloured beads, glass and various ornaments are used. Tinkling bells are tied to the legs. OTTAMTHULLAL is distinct with its presentation and frank wit and humour. This dance form is a solo dance performance. The dancer himself sings the lead to the accompaniment of instruments. The metre, and rhythm of OTTAMTHULLAL songs are fast-paced. The face of the dancer is painted green, lips painted red and the eyes are emphasised with black.

KUTHIYOTTAM

In the southern parts of Kerala boys perform this folk dance. The dancers draw colourful spots on their faces and wear crowns and ornaments. The dancers also carry round discs when they perform the dance with quick movements. Singers also sing songs in the background.

MARGOMKALI

It is an entertainment popularized by Syrian Christians. The dance is performed around a brass lamp (Nilavilakku) with lighted oil wicks. The rhythmic steps synchronised with the rhythm and tune of the song are similar to those used in Thiruvathirakali.

KAKKARISSI NATAKAM

This folk drama is performed by artists living in Trivandrum district and in the area surrounding it. It is a folk theatre art meant for entertainment. One Thampuran (Lord) asks questions and Kakkalan gives answers. Their dialogues present brazen faced criticism of the contemporary society.

POORAM

The most spectacular of these is Thrissur Pooram the annual temple festival in Trichur. Held in April – May, it includes a spectacular procession of ten temple deities. Some thirty caparisoned elephants of a uniform size move in row. Atop them sit Brahmin priests under silk parasols.

The procession winds its way through the streets throughout the day to the accompaniment of ritual music, while devotees make offering of rice and flowers. The Pooram begins with elephant processions from minor temples moving gracefully to the Vadukumnathan temple and march out after paying respects to

Lord VADAKUMNATHAN. Following sunset, the spectacle is again enacted, this time is accompanied by flaming torches and fireworks, and heralded by the roll of drums. For those who would like to participate in concerts, this is the time for some of the finest KATHAKALI performances and Carnatic music recitals. The highlight of THRISSUR POORAM is the KOODIKAZHCHA of the deities of PARAMELKAVU and THIRUVAMBADY temples and the famous KUDAMATTOM or exchange of colourful umbrellas.

ONAM

ONAM, the main festival of Kerala is a celebration lasting 10 days. You find every Keralite in a rejoicing mood. ONAM in August – September is Kerala's harvest festival and New Year celebration.

People get their homes painted, wear new clothes, make floral decorations in the courtyards to greet King MAHABALI, whose legendary rule signifies prosperity. It is believed that King MAHABALI visits every home to see the welfare of the people. The legend says that he was pushed down to the nether world by VAMANA, an incarnation of Lord VISHNU but was given a boon that he could visit his erstwhile kingdom once in a year on the ONAM day. The snake boat race that are held at Kottayam, ARANMULA and PAYIPAD in the backwaters make this festival truly enjoyable for the people of the whole state.

The traditional feast of Kerala- called SADYA- steps is dished up readily during ONAM, in every restaurant or home. Exotically served on a clean fresh banana leaf, this multi-course extravaganza comprise mainly rice and countless vegetarian curries and dishes. And most of them are coconut based.

With various tongue-tingling pickles adding that touch of spice, and topped by large helpings of PAYASAMS - (sweet milky porridge served with dried fruits and nuts) the feast represents the prosperity during the legendary rule of king MAHABHALI.

YOGA

Ancient Indian wisdom has given the key to mental peace, radiant health and spiritual fulfilment amidst the intense stress of modern life. This key is the practical science of YOGA.

YOGA is a timeless means of integrating individuals, regardless of their physical, cultural or spiritual characteristics, so that they can manifest peace and health in their daily lives, here and now.

It is immensely practical and has nothing to do with superstitions. Yoga has lasted throughout the thousands of years of Indian culture and has now firmly taken room in western countries as well. Its simplicity is sublime and its essence lies in its practical nature.

AYURVEDA

Ayurveda is the ancient Indian health science developed through centuries long research works of sages, who were eminent scholars. As the term AYURVEDA denotes to 'the knowledge of life' it is not only a system to cure disease but a system teaching us how to achieve 'Perfect Health' from diseased or abnormal conditions and how to lead our lives, both physical and mental, to attain the bliss or real life. The Tourism Department of Kerala has now packaged tours to show stunning scenery- including lakes, seas, forest, hills, tea plantations, spice groves and sanctuaries-and laced them with adventure tourism, the monsoons and Ayurveda as the end product in its tourism promotion drive. The beauty of monsoons can be fully savoured when a tourist undergoes Ayurveda therapy which restricts his movements and hence leaves him free to relish the rhythm of the rains.

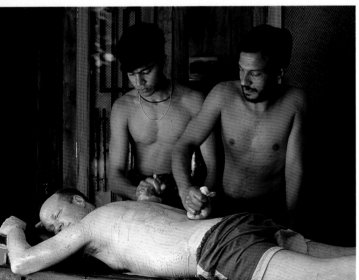

Kerala has a special type of AYURVEDA treatment. Though the texts of lessons studied are same the system of treatment is entirely different and far more effective as well. These special Kerala treatments include PIZHICHIL (Oil bath), ILAKIZHI (leaf bundle massage), NAVARAKIZHI (rice bundle massage) etc; which are widely and effectively used in the treatment of chronic severe illnesses such as rheumatoid arthritis, paralysis, facial palsy, motor neuron disease, ankylosing spondylitis, acute infective polyneuritis, various spinal problems, gastric or peptic ulcers etc.

Kerala has a soothing climate with natural abundance of forests with a wealth of herbs and medicinal plants. Kerala is the only state in India, where this system of medicine is practised with absolute dedication.

The martial art of Karate is believed to have evolved from Kalaripayattu.

KALARIPPAYATTU

KALARIPPAYATTU is a form of martial arts. Regular practice of KALARIPPAYATTU can make a person healthy and energetic. Many well known experts of KALARIPPAYATTU in Kerala are now a days offering training in this martial art. The tourists from distant places such as Spain reach EDAKKAD, a suburb of KOZHIKODE city to learn KALARIPPAYATTU. According to a Swede who reached India to study Odissi and folk arts, KALARIPPAYATTU is also useful for dancers. The opinion is shared by many who perform various dance forms and all of them believe that the movements of Kalarippayattu enhance the appeal for the dance. The MARMACHIKITSA a treatment system developed along with KALARIPPAYATTU involves applying pressure on 107 nodal points in the human body to correct muscular and neurological problems.

KERALA CUISINE

Kerala offers several gastronomic opportunities. Spices that flavour the local cuisine give it a sharp pungency that is heightened with the use of tamarind, while coconut gives it its richness absorbing some of the tongue – teasing, pepper-hot flavours. In most part of South India, there is a tendency towards vegetarian restaurants. However there is a good deal of sea food available, and the prawn curries in their beds of coconut gravy are exceptionally good. Curries are eaten usually with plain steamed rice. Small steamed rice cakes called IDALIS and the crepe-like pancakes called DOSAS served with CHUTNEY and SAMBAR are the usual menu for a typical breakfast. Other delicacies include APPAM a puffy variation of DOSA (fermented coconut-water or toddy is mixed for making APPAM) and can be had either with egg masala or chicken curry.

The hotels in the larger towns serve a medley of international cuisines too, and these include Chinese as well as selected Continental delicacies.

PEOPLE AND LIFESTYLE

People of Kerala have a history replete with important events that brought about drastic changes in their social conditions and religious beliefs. Since the formation of the state, the disparities between castes and communities have disappeared. Rapid urbanisation has helped the villages to have modern amenities. People have become more and more conscious about their social status. The remittances from Keralites who live and work in gulf countries helped to improve the standard of living of people. New mansions with marble floors are seen even in remote parts of villages. In cities and towns vehicular traffic has increased and more and more people are using their own cars and scooters. The tradition bound society in Kerala seems to have opened its doors to modern concepts of globalization. Large scale computerisation has widened the area of business transactions. Keralites are gradually acquiring a life style for themselves that gives them the true identity of people who would like to explore hitherto unknown spheres of luxurious living.

Kallu shop- you could visit one of the thatched toddy shops for a glass of the fermented beverage (Toddy) which is served with delicious fried 'Crab' or KARIMEEN a fish that is special gift of these backwaters.

Just married- posing for a photograph.

Munnar- offers the best view of tea plantations.